DARK
HIGHWAY

Utah's Strange Tales

Dan Kenyon

iUniverse, Inc.
Bloomington

Dark Highway
Utah's Strange Tales

Copyright © 2010 Dan Kenyon

iUniverse books may be ordered through booksellers or by contacting:

iUniverse
1663 Liberty Drive
Bloomington, IN 47403
www.iuniverse.com
1-800-Authors (1-800-288-4677)

ISBN: 978-1-4502-2706-3 (pbk)
ISBN: 978-1-4502-2705-6 (ebk)

Printed in the United States of America

iUniverse rev. date: 12/1/2010

Cover photo by Daniel Johnson

To my mother—she supported every creative endeavor I ever attempted, and as a foster grandparent, she supports the hopes and dreams of the next several generations.

My wife, Amy, and daughter, Emily Mae—either waiting for me to get home or go to bed, they always made home a great place to get to.

Richard Johnson, my late father-in-law—he set an example as a lifelong learner and was always interested; therefore, he was always interesting. Rest in peace.

Thanks to (Alien) Dave Rosenfeld of the Utah UFO Hunters and the trips to look at the night sky. Thanks, also, to Marlee Spendlove, assistant director of the Salt Lake MUFON branch.

I wrote this book in five years while rebuilding a house, holding down a forty-hour-per-week job and helping chase my daughter around. I couldn't have done this without Candace Sinclair of "The Writer's Mentor." Her experience saves me time and she answers e-mail like a proper human being.

The staff at the Salt Lake City Library are overworked and underpaid. I may be too old to give a "shout out," so I'll just say "thank you."

To those poor souls who think no one is listening—look up, down, or around—maybe "they" are.

Acknowledgments

Ever since I was a kid in Vermont and watched out for "Champ" on Lake Champlain and the classic "Mansi" photo of the lake creature graced the front page of the *New York Times*. I've been fascinated by the paranormal.

Reading Joe Citro's *Green Mountain Ghosts and Ghouls* kept me looking for the spirits of the dead in covered bridges and old barns.

When I got married and settled in Utah, I became interested in what was happening here in the "twilight zone."

I started going to local Mutual UFO Network (MUFON) meetings and joined the Utah UFO Hunters. "Alien" Dave Rosenfeld is the director of this group. He's knowledgeable and creative. I've talked to him about his own UFO sightings while we were on sky watches or at meetings.

He has built an incredible Web site that has been a major source of guidance and information. It has given me fast insight into Utah's varied landscape.

As the assistant director, Marlee Spendlove organizes the MUFON meetings. She does a great job and the meetings are always interesting.

Salt Lake City's library is a great hall of knowledge; it's a piece of art where people can study in peace. I found a number of great books, including Frank Salisbury's *The Utah UFO Display* and Marie Jones' *PSIence: How New Discoveries in Quantum Physics and New Science May Explain the Existence of Paranormal Phenomena*.

Other books that had me burning the midnight tungsten were *Time Storms: Amazing Evidence for Time Warps, Space Rifts, and Time Travel* by Jenny Randles. John White's *Pole Shift* made me worry about my compass.

I learned to question the human timeline while reading *The Hidden History of the Human Race* by Michael A. Cremo and Richard L. Thompson.

Ghosts in America's haunted hotels were covered by Frances Kerman's *Ghostly Encounters: True Stories of America's Haunted Hotels*.

I read about UFO sightings in the last fifty years by the military and airline professionals, including government documents that were collected by Timothy Good in *Above Top Secret: The Worldwide UFO Cover-Up*.

I also learned a lot about everything paranormal from the speakers at the UFO Congress in Laughlin, Nevada. Keynote speaker Richard Dolan is a hard-to-ignore researcher and author.

Finally, the creepy events surrounding the piece of ground called "the UFO Ranch," among other things, was recounted in the gripping *Hunt for the Skinwalker: Science Confronts the Unexplained at a Remote Ranch in Utah"* by Colm A. Kelleher, PhD and George Knapp.

There is still a lot to figure out and I hope to keep delving in and asking myself, *What if?* All while having a little good, clean fun.

Contents

Introduction

This book is a look into the strange and sometimes silly things that happen in the state of Utah, which is known for skiing, rock climbing, the Osmonds, and the Olympics. Most people don't know the half of it, but now they will know the "rest of the story."

You will learn about the UFOs that fly through the skies, the ghosts that inhabit very old buildings, and things that move across the land that go unnoticed in the dark. Utah has places that have no explanation for what happens there, leaving professional scientists walking away and scratching their heads.

Cattle are mutilated with no evidence to work with and canyon walls change around travelers and place them in another dimension, hunted by who knows what.

The Utah UFO Hunters were on the scene, investigating what they could. In the "UFO Ranch," several members camped on the road nearby and went through inexplicable sensations and events. They observed firefly-like lights moving over the ground, but Utah doesn't have fireflies.

Utah is beautiful, but it's also full of mystery. This world may not be so easy to figure out, but it's far from boring.

CHAPTER 1

Spirits

It's funny what people will do for status. Take the case of John Baptiste. He was simply a humble "grave digger" when Salt Lake City was only a town. He was always well dressed and financially able.

However, everything was not as it seemed. Mr. Baptiste had been placed under surveillance by the police. A man from back East had traveled to Utah to have the body of a deceased relative exhumed and brought back with him to be buried there. When checking inside the coffin, they discovered a completely nude body, face down and devoid of any jewelry.

One day, someone spotted Mr. Baptiste pushing a wheelbarrow with a nude body. They followed him and watched as he dumped it in front of a grave. If you thought "grave digger" carries a stigma, try "grave robber."

The police were informed of the incident and an investigation revealed that John Baptiste had done this to thousands of people whom he had buried.

Inside his house, clothes were dumped over furniture and draped over windows. In the basement, a large pot of clothes gurgled along at a boil. He not only took their money and personal belongings, he also took any memories of dignity their families might have had. Relatives came forward to confirm whether the graves of their loved ones had been disturbed.

There was a speedy trial and John Baptiste was found guilty. He was subsequently banished to Stansbury Island (within sight of Antelope Island on the Great Salt Lake).

The authorities left him there with food, water, and limited supplies. He was told that a parole officer would check on him. However, of course, these stories always end this way. When he was checked on a few weeks later, he was gone. Whether he had made a raft or swam away, John Baptiste had escaped a tedious, lonely fate. In the end, he had been relegated to a dubious local legend. Some say they have seen a ghost wandering on the shores of Great Salt Lake, solemnly clutching a pile of rotting clothes.

Desert Spirits

The first ghost I ever saw was Casper the Friendly Ghost, But he was more goofy than scary. No one knows for sure what "they" are, but more than 65 percent of Americans believe that "they" are real. Whether ghosts take the full form of a real person in their appearance—as a floating ball of light or a force invisible to the eye—they make their presence known.

The sightings go back centuries—in every culture and country. Apparitions have been seen on land and sea, in creaky old buildings, and, of course, where the dead quietly rest. In modern times, technology and those astute in applying it have stepped in to take inaccurate perceptions out of the equation. Electrical charges can be measured and cold spots detected—along with infrared spectrum photography to measure forms unseen by the naked eye. Electronic Voice Phenomenon (EVP) records the rather unsettling sounds that are not heard by investigators when they are recording, but that are audible when the tapes are replayed. How something without vocal chords can produce a voice is just one of many questions facing investigators as they document their findings.

Utah is a state loaded with history and spirits. No less than five Indian tribes roamed the land; travelers from the East Coast looked for a place to call home and found it in the mid-1800s. The rough country was settled by hearty pioneers—mostly Mormons—plus a dose of cowboys, military, immigrants, and adventurous mountain men to name a few. Utah was a state for the tough; they all faced hardship and often died from illness or violence well before middle age. A town was started at the base of the Wasatch Mountains, bordered by a vast salt lake, and it grew from there.

This is a collection of sightings from the Beehive State. There is no shortage of material. I have culled through many accounts and have narrowed them down to a few varied and well-known collections of things that can't seem to "move on."

The Old Mill

The Old Mill is one of the most haunted buildings in Utah. Located right next to a road, it is gothic, out of place, and grimly refuses to conform to the development around it.

It was a resort in its better days in the 1920s—a place where people went to get away from the bustle of the big city. Evolving into a restaurant in the 1970s—still plagued with odd problems such as fire—it went through the disco phase. By the 1980s, it was a Halloween spook house. Little did most people know that there was something real to that title.

Many people have died there, including an infamous suicide by gunshot that took place in the morbidly named "heart room." The man was not found for months and the bloodstain remained untouched long after the gruesome discovery.

Jimmy Chunga, a local actor and radio personality, was a security guard at the time. He remembers some very creepy things that happened in the spook alley and says the place is evil. One time, while walking down a flight of stairs alone, his radio power repeatedly went out. This was a constant problem. A door he had just gone through slammed shut and his flashlight turned off. Since that was a chronic problem, guards often carried extra batteries in their cargo pockets.

The door would not open and he was alone. He had no signal from his radio and no light. The six-foot-five security guard got a little freaked.

He says, "To this day, the place is bad. No one should try to break in."

Chunga also recalls a time when a paranormal investigator wanted to spend the night inside alone —just him and his equipment. Even though he was warned, the cameras, temperature sensors, and sound recorders were hauled inside. After a short time, he walked out and left the pricey gear behind.

Violent fires have ravaged the building over the years. Two transients died on the grounds and I believe their dog died also.

Now, it's supposedly deemed unsafe to go inside due to structural reasons, but people in the know have a real reason— it's spiritually unsafe. If evil has a home, this is it.

In the last decade or so, it is only used for the occasional exterior shot in the odd movie production and is gated the rest of the time. The windows are bolted and marked "off limits." Nevertheless, every Halloween, the curious and the foolhardy make their way to try to get a look or feel of a building that is not just a building, but also one that "breathes" in a hoarse groan and has a bloody heart.

The Ghost of Elbow Fork

My wife, Amy, and her friend had an unsettling experience while hiking up Elbow Fork Trail several years ago. Since the trail and the day were beautiful, it only took about twenty minutes for them to get to the top.

At the top, they came to a clearing where they had to walk through a tree-lined area. As they made their way to the clearing, Amy saw an old man sitting approximately five to six feet off the trail under a pine tree.

He had white hair and no beard or glasses. He wore a red shirt with gray pants and had only one leg. He was staring right through her. Amy, taken a bit off guard by the sight, did not say hello. Her friend, Kathleen, didn't say anything either. They continued to walk for fifty yards or so back to the clearing.

They looked at each other and said, "Did you see that?"

After a moment, they turned and went back down the trail to confirm what they had seen. However, they couldn't find him anywhere. They searched around the brush in the surrounding area, but there were no tracks and no sign of anything or any other hikers on the trail. They had been alone.

Now jump ahead a couple of years. Amy and I were taking a hike up that very same trail. We were taking in the sights and talking about the strange old ghost. We came to the spot where she had originally seen him. It was very close to the trail and not on some distant hillside. We walked the fifty yards to the turnaround point and headed back down the trail. After 150 or so yards, something caught my attention. It wasn't a vision because I couldn't see anything in particular. I felt something was out of my view—something dark behind a branch. Amy saw it too. I stepped off the trail and attempted to move it with my walking stick.

I casually reached for the branch and moved it aside. Behind the dead brown pine branch was a black foot brace. It was shin length and its sole looked to be made of wood. We paused for a moment because it was a little odd.

When I went to pick up the brace for examination, my wife shrieked a bit loudly. Using my trusty walking stick, I tried to move the creepy brace and found it was nailed to the tree! That's right. For some strange reason, someone had hiked up the trail with a leg brace, nailed it to a tree, broke off a pine bough, and laid it carefully in front of it.

It was a Sunday and strangely no one else was on the trail—but the trail on the north side had plenty of people on it. I share my account because it's a case of odd synchronicity—not because I believe that a ghost left a leg brace behind.

I've not heard another account of the ghost of Elbow Fork. If you find yourself up there and see an old man appearing as real as anyone, staring at you on the trail, say "hello."

Soldier Clem

Fort Douglas is a fun place to visit if you like old things. It's located on the northeast side of Salt Lake City, sitting comfortably along the foothills for 140 years or so. The museum was established in 1974. People can wander around, examine historical weapons, and check out the "cannon park."

One time, a curious sightseer walked up to a man in charge and asked who that authentic-looking "actor" was in the period-piece costume. He had seen the man earlier leaning up against the porch railing and casually smoking a pipe.

The man answered, "We don't have actors in costume—never have. That was probably Clem. He makes an appearance every so often."

I visited there on Halloween a couple of years ago. They had a "Ghost of Fort Douglas" presentation that night. I found out they have more than one ghost residing there, but it seems that Clem decided to take the night off.

A Capitol Theater Inhabitant

The old theater was a palace in its day; built with careful attention to last a long time. It still shines in the present when it hosts plays and operas. The story of what or who turns off lights and slams doors, starts with the story of Jim. Jim, a stagehand working at the theater in the 1940s, died suddenly one day from a bad fall. Ever since, generations of witnesses have attested to the fact that the electrical system has a mind of its own. Ghost investigators have been in the theater and noticed very cold spots, recorded EVP, and photographed "orbs." No one has attempted to exorcise the spirit due to the fact that, like many benign entities, they don't terrify the inhabitants.

Black Ectoplasm

About ten years ago, when I still lived in Vermont, I was going to a Halloween party dressed as the adult version of Eddie Munster. I even made a teddy bear I called "Wolfie."

My friend Billy picked me up and we were driving in the sunset near a local cemetery. I looked off to the side and asked Bill if he had his camera in the van.

He said, "Sure."

I suggested that we pull over and get some shots of my costume while we had a great location and lighting.

This cemetery has a great crypt door built into the hillside; the entryway roof is rounded and covered with grass like a hobbit house. He took some pictures of me by the crypt's old wooden door and by some graves. About a month later, I stopped at Billy's house to check out the shots. They were printed on a "one sheet" that shows small versions of all the shots we had taken.

Most of the pictures were of local older buildings that Billy liked to photograph. They all turned out nice—each in different lighting conditions with black and white film.

However, the pictures of me were all fogged out. They couldn't have been exposed since they were in the middle of a roll and only within my frames. Billy is too good a photographer to have had a dirty lens or to have put his thumb in the frame.

It was very strange that a "black cloud" appeared only on my cemetery photos. Years later, I asked Barbara of the Ghost Investigation Society (G.I.S.) if there was such a thing as "black ectoplasm."

She answered, "Yes, I've seen it many times."

The Forgotten

Utah's Gold Spike area is important historically as the joining of the railroad from the East to the West. It's rough country—rolling hills, cattle, and sheep ranches—and was probably difficult "rocky progress" in the day. Many men gave their lives to complete this huge effort—many of whom would never be remembered. Most all of them were Chinese immigrants, but some were black and some were convicts.

A century later on a dark night, a train engineer was scanning the tracks ahead for animals, trees, or other trains that might be a danger. He was about to be tested.

He saw a single light in the distance coming toward his engine. He pulled hard on the whistle and started braking—even though he knew he wouldn't make it in time. He couldn't understand how the other train had gotten so close.

Staring through the gloom, he tried to make out the other engine. The light started to fade more and more as it approaches—and then it was gone!

The Rio Grande

The Rio Grande has a restaurant, holds the occasional small concert, and is cohabitated by ghosts. The old station no longer houses passengers and is no longer a bustling hub.

The "Lady in Purple" still wears perfume, seems attached to the ladies room, and wears a purple dress. She died on the tracks—struck down by a train while she tried to retrieve a ring thrown down by an angry suitor.

In the 1980s, witnesses could hear footsteps on the balcony above and made out the figure of a man walking in the lobby. Hearing loud party sounds in the basement, security took the elevator to the source of the fun, expecting to shut it down. When the doors parted, a puzzled guard stared into what his senses told him that he could not believe: an empty, silent room.

Face of Emo

Jacob Moritz is the name on the crypt in the Salt Lake Cemetery, but everybody knows him as "Emo." It is said that if you carry a lighted candle and walk around the "tower" at midnight, you will see Emo's face in the small window on the front. There is no guarantee of it, but a lot of people go on the Halloween ghost tour to give it a try. It's at least worth a visit to the Salt Lake Cemetery to view this strange monolith.

It turns out that there is nothing really scary about the real Jacob Moritz. In the late 1800s, the successful businessman had started the Salt Lake Brewing Company. He was married to the same woman for many years, donated back to the city, and even helped victims of the San Francisco earthquake.

He was respected by the members of the Mormon Church for being a fair-minded man and died in Germany on vacation with his wife. His ashes were brought home and sealed in the famous tomb.

The Victim of the Beast

What would make a person want to have "Victim of the beast" chiseled their gravestone? The name on the tombstone is Lillian Gray, but everyone talks about the dark hint at her demise. Her husband was buried with an ordinary marker in a different part of the cemetery.

Mrs. Gray was born in June of 1881 and died in November of 1958. Gravestones aren't free. It seems unlikely that someone would order an epitaph with no meaning, but no one seems to be left alive to explain it.

The City County Building

The City County Building in downtown Salt Lake is a classic example of Gothic architecture. On the building's grounds (comprised of several acres), many festivals and events have and still occur. The fact that the building is haunted by five ghosts doesn't seem to make a difference.

Two children were believed to have died during its construction—a brother and sister. Also, the mother's ghost is thought to float through the floors—maybe she's looking for her children. All five floors are haunted. Security guards often report cold spots, lights going on and off, and children laughing.

The "clunk" of a ghost of a pioneer judge's wooden leg can be heard echoing throughout the halls—as well as a former mayor's ghost. Tunnels below the building have also proven active; EVP has been recorded and orbs have been witnessed.

The Ben Lomond Hotel

Built in 1891, this hotel in Ogden, Utah, has a rich history and still has guests—some alive and some not so alive. Many people who work there know the stories about Room 1102— the room haunted by a spectral woman waiting for her son to return from World War II. He never came back, but she is still there. Suicides occurred in the hotel and many managers and staff have seen, heard, and felt the presence of something or someone.

A cleaning woman vacuuming in Room 1102 was reaching under the bed when she felt something holding onto the vacuum, not wanting to release it. Others have seen a smoke-like apparition on the stairs and in the tunnels below the hotel. It's active with live people back in the early "party days." Being a bit of a wide-open town, it now often has "orbs" moving about. Schoolchildren on tours of the tunnels often see orbs—lots of them—through the camera viewfinder.

Activity followed the schoolchildren to the upstairs rooms and one child got more than his share of thrills. He was actually pushed from behind—even though no human was there.

Lights go on and off, the tub in 1102 fills on its own sometimes, and the elevator travels and stays on the floor of its own choosing. Nevertheless, this is still a working hotel and restaurant with a popular piano bar. If you don't mind the possibility of unexpected company, I recommend you stay there.

Wandering Nephites

The Nephites were conquered around AD 600 by their longtime enemies, the lamanites. However, an old Mormon legend tells of three still wandering around. The tale goes back about 150 years. Pioneers would be visited by three wandering Nephites. They appeared needy—or at least hungry—and without means. They were offered help. They would accept the neighborly gesture of food and water and then would say goodbye and leave. A meal of fresh bread and meat was found left behind for the generous family, without explanation. It must have happened often enough because the tale survives to this day.

The Ghost of Brigham's Wife

Brigham Young—one of the original Mormon pioneers in Salt Lake City—had more than one wife. One of those wives, Mary, died fairly young, yet might be seen to this day. Her huge house is an historic building and was moved to the This Is The Place Heritage Park—a sentiment expressed when pioneers found the valley. Cold spots are felt even in hot weather, doors slam, and Mary has been seen in the window shaking her finger at children she still believes that she's in charge of.

The Old Utah County Jail

The Utah County Jail is over a hundred years old and it creaks and groans as if it's worked for every one of those. Today it's closed, but it had its share of unsavory visitors that still move about and make themselves known. Voices can be heard and recorded on E.V.P.

One ghost investigator caught a warning on his recorder that said, "Get out of here!"

CHAPTER 2
Unidentified Flying Objects

They moved silently, gliding back and forth as stark searchlights moved over the desert field and then the road. James, his wife, and family dog were traveling to visit some friends in Wilmington.

After driving for some time, they encountered something right out of a movie. They described them as a "triangle and disk moving as a pair" flying above the road. The couple was driving or gliding at about five hundred feet. A search beam glowed from the bottom of each—sweeping as though looking for something.

The dog in the back seat bared its teeth and growled. Every time the objects moved toward the road, the dog howled as if it was being stabbed. This went on for twenty minutes.

When the couple got home, they had a tough time sleeping. Even the dog would look out the window and up at the sky as if to check whether it was safe before reluctantly sleeping on its bed.

This was not the family's first encounter with UFOs. They still have frequent nightmares and the dog is still clearly affected by what it saw. The sighting was reported on the

UUFOH's Web site and it's a little unique due to multiple witnesses and craft.

Unidentified flying objects—UFOs—bring to mind many preconceived notions that I don't like to use, but I try to stick to the first accurate, original definition.

The Uintah Basin

In the 1960s and 1970s, there were a large number of UFO sightings in the Uintah Basin. At the time, Frank Salisbury was doing the research for his book, *The Utah UFO Display*. He was a trained biologist and investigated the sightings very methodically. He befriended and interviewed members of the local Indian tribe who lived at the reservation. A lot of "legwork" and interviewing skills were also carried out by his friend and assistant, Mr. Junior Hicks.

From these witnesses, combined with reports of the local longtime families of the area, he documented the sightings and gathered drawings to build an impressive body of work. These witnesses were ordinary people—working class—and many were members of the Mormon Church.

Although there was a high amount of activity in the area, Salisbury never witnessed a UFO while he was in the Roosevelt, Ouray, and Vernal areas. This didn't make him doubt the witnesses, but it illustrates the importance of being in the right place at the right time.

Sighting #1

On Labor Day weekend of 1967, bow hunters made their way down a rain-soaked back road that rambled past pinion pines. Buck Canyon was their final destination, having left from Ouray and settling in for the ride. They expected an uneventful and boring commute. How wrong they were! They passed over rolling hills and approached a sharp dugway.

Up ahead on the road—and in the mud—was a truck loaded with cedar rails. Gasoline was still bleeding from the engine.

Even the wheels still dripped mud. One thing was blaringly apparent. No driver—injured or not—could be seen. The area around the truck showed no tracks or marks. Since the vehicle was headed the same direction, the hunters should have seen someone coming back their way. They had seen no one.

They felt very strange at that scene, but didn't stay to speculate. They hoped they would spot someone walking ahead and they carried on.

Rising and dipping, the road gave a peek-a-boo view of the horizon off to the right. Albertson glimpsed what looked like a fire, but it appeared to be moving.

He stopped the truck on the crest of the hill. Sure enough, something was moving along with the horizon. Then he saw it sink down, not moving for a few seconds, and then it rose powerfully straight up and out of sight.

They might've forgotten something because it came down in a different location. Hovering still, they felt as if they were being watched. Then it came much faster than the first time. It snapped upward and was gone.

After five days, they checked with the sheriff's office, but nothing had turned up and there was no missing persons report.

Maybe the person traveled with others and went on with them. Maybe he was forced off the road by a careless pilot from another planet. We will never know.

Sighting #2

Czar Rudy was returning from Flaming Gorge with his son on

October 1967. Seeing what they thought was a haystack on fire, they drove on and approached the object for a better look.

It began to move upward as they drew near. They could see it was a "half saucer" and it glowed more like tumbleweed. The light was intense as it rose up to the size of a harvest moon. It was totally silent.

Stopping the car to watch, it made a circle moving northwest. The father got on top of the car and saw a hard edge on the bottom of the red half disk before it disappeared.

Sighting # 3

Driving from Vernal to Roosevelt on a spring evening in 1967, Tony Zufelt and his wife noticed a glow growing brighter around the car. Frantically, they looked in every direction and finally looked up.

Only an estimated 150 feet up, something passed over the road as if headed for Vernal.
It eerily remained silent. Tony described it as looking like a tapered boxcar complete with window and orbs of light floating out the back—more "like doors than windows"—maybe ten feet tall and getting smaller toward the rear of the object.

A bluish flame lit each "window" and the estimated length of the craft passed in front of him maybe 150 feet long. Now, it was so low to the ground that they couldn't see under it.

Once they got home, they called his father-in-law. The ten o'clock news said that a police officer in Colorado had reported a similar sighting.

The Ranch Puzzle

That calf will be perfectly safe, he thought. Heck, he'd only be gone for ten or fifteen minutes and would only be short distance away. When he got back to the area where he'd left the calf, he noticed all the cows huddled to one side of the corral. The remains were gruesome. Tom Gorman couldn't believe his eyes—the poor animal had been drawn and quartered. *How could something tear the animal apart without a sound in so short a time and in such close proximity?* The other animals were obviously spooked by this latest example of the dark and mysterious forces at work on this cursed property.

The ranch in question had been sold to the Gorman family in the early 1990s. Tom Gorman was a bull breeder and planned to raise and sell bulls there. The family thought they could enjoy the beautiful rugged area of eastern Utah.

Again and again, they found that they were assailed by a variety of phenomena. If they had asked the local Indian tribe, they would have discovered that the land was uninhabitable.

Not only did cattle mutilation occur, but UFOs, poltergeists, and psychic effects took place, including what the Indians refer to as "skinwalkers" (more on those later).

One evening as they were settling in to the property, the family was in the driveway. Something that looked like a dog was moving toward them. As it got closer, it appeared larger and dark. They watched as it moved closer. Since it was a working ranch, they had firearms nearby and were ready.

The mother took the children inside as the large "wolf dog" moved closer. It casually walked up to the rancher and sniffed at his hand. The wolf's shoulder came up to Tom Gorman's waist. The still-cautious family calmed a bit as the hound ambled to the edge of the calf pen. A calf stuck its head through the rail. In one quick motion, the wolf lurched forward and clamped onto the calf's snout.

The rancher reacted quickly, taking a board and striking the wolf with full force. The creature didn't seem to notice much, but eventually released the frightened calf. Slowly, the wolf turned to leave.

Then a pistol was used at close range, but had no lasting

effect. Tom's brother used a 30.06 rifle as it moved off, but the animal only jumped slightly. The high-powered shell impacted, but the wolf continued to walk into the distance. Upon following and looking for tracks, they found no blood trail as the tracks led to a muddy bog-like area. The tracks just stopped as if the creature had floated away.

Cat and Mouse

One night when Tom and his son were checking the perimeter of the fence, they saw two taillights in the distance. Occasionally, on large property, someone hunting, fishing, or joyriding crossed the line and became a trespasser. Usually you only had to talk to them and let them know where they were before they would leave all the wiser.

They followed the taillights farther along the road. Closer to the end of the property, they left their truck behind and started to run to catch up as the taillights floated in the distance. As they closed in, the two lights moved up, flew over the fence and the hill without a pause or trace.

They were again confronted with events that they couldn't—and decidedly wouldn't—explain. They shook their heads and walked back to the truck.

The Triangle

The Black Triangles had been seen on the ranch before. On this particular night, Ellen was driving home. Tom was out of town and she was planning to spend the night by herself. Considering what had already happened, she wasn't looking forward to it.

It was a clear, quiet night and she looked up to the stars as something caught her eye. The stars were blackened out and a series of red, blue, green, and yellow lights illuminated the bottom of a large triangular object that was silently pacing her vehicle from less than fifty feet above.

She was frightened—as anyone might be—and tried to focus on the road. She only wanted to get home. The triangle moved away from the driveway and Ellen quickly went inside. After trying to settle down and digest a meal, she gazed out at the corral from the window over the kitchen sink. What struck her as odd was what appeared to be a darkly shadowed object *inside* the corral. A light inside the shape almost looked as if it was some sort of camper.

As she tried to find some explanation, she thought, *What would someone be doing camping in a stranger's corral?* It looked as if there was an object inside resembling a desk with a dark figure sitting at it.

She could not make out many details of this person—except the stranger was dressed all in black. It proceeded to stand in the doorway of what she realized was the triangle craft she had seen on her way home.

The tall figure stood blocking the door and staring straight at her. Her hands shook as she reached to grab the shade and cover the window. She reached for the phone. Tom was hours away, but the fear and tension in her voice persuaded him to return home immediately.

Tom tried to calm her when he got there at daylight. They looked around together for clues. The large footprints were unlike any he'd seen before—no tread, smooth, with a round heel, and about eighteen inches long. Whoever it was didn't shop at Payless and, as usual, provided far more questions than answers.

Strange Contact

When enough weird things happen at a ranch in a relatively

small town, word gets out. That's why Tom was quietly cautious when a pickup truck rolled down their unmarked driveway.

The man got out and walked toward Tom. He quickly greeted Tom and his son and said that he didn't mean to bother them. He didn't want to ask any questions, he only wanted to meditate—that's right, *meditate*—on his property.

Tom would never have imagined that a stranger would want that and it threw him a little. As the man explained, he only wanted to sit somewhere on the property and meditate.

The request seemed innocent enough and Tom agreed.

He led the man to a field and the man settled his large frame cross-legged on the grass. Off in the trees, Tom and his son saw a movement about two hundred yards away. It had no shape—only a movement that shifted through the trees. Then without hesitation, it broke from the trees and moved over open ground several feet in the air—directly toward the visitor.

Before they could even shout a warning, the large blurry object stopped a short distance away and let out a roar. This shocked everyone. Like an intense animal roar, the force alone stunned the seated man and rolled him backward. The blurred apparition whirled around and zipped back to the trees. The shocked man rose to his feet, assisted by Tom and his son. He became a blubbering mess, clutching in fear, and unable to let go until Tom finally threatened violence. After he let go, they helped him slowly get back into his truck. His face was as gray as concrete.

The truck sped off almost too quickly and Tom thought that he might have an accident on his hands. However, after a few shaky turns, they watched the truck enter the main road.

Later as the father and son were relaxing and watching a movie, they jumped up at the image on the screen—neither could believe their eyes. The movie was "Predator" with Arnold Schwarzenegger, but they both were staring at the creature that was a camouflaged star of the movie—that was what they had seen cross the field, threatening the meditating man with its sonic howl.

The Last Straw

Everyone has a limit and the Gormans finally hit theirs. Tom was relaxing on the porch, but it wouldn't last long. Once again, a feeling in his gut evolved into apprehension. Watching the tree line, he caught sight of a glowing orange orb moving through the trees at a high rate of speed. *It's happening again,* he thought.

It darted here and there smoothly. The three dogs sitting at Tom's feet took sharp notice and growled, tensing for anything. They all stood and watched as it floated about. The dogs couldn't resist. This was some kind of invader and they were determined to guard the property.

Tom finally gave the signal. Off they went after it as it swooped away low and toward the hills. Tom stood as he grew concerned. It seemed to tease the dogs, darting downward at them and then up at the last second. It led the dogs over a hilltop. They ran over to the dip below and Tom heard an awful noise—intense, loud, panicked barks—and then nothing. Tom bolted off the porch, running over the hill and down toward the trees in the gully. No dogs could be seen. As he approached, the orange orb was gone, but he saw the large circular patches of charred remains of his three faithful companions.

Absolutely sickened and brokenhearted, Tom called it quits. He gathered his family and moved off this troubled land, deciding they would try to sell the property.

The National Institute of Discovery Science (NIDS) Arrives

After Tom and his family moved, the story of the ranch went "national." Much covered by George Knapp, a Nevada reporter with staunch character and rare integrity. He wanted to see that the story got attention—even though it didn't involve any Hollywood divas, models, or heiresses. The subject matter also ruined careers.

NIDS is the only organization of scientists who possess the stones—no, not enchanted stones—to investigate something unexplained but so important.

Not to get off track, but I heard on the radio the other day about researchers studying whether chimp babies need nutrition or nurturing.

They wired together a "mommy" monkey with a milk bottle sticking out. It was essentially a monkey-shaped cage with a milk bottle. Then they made a cage with fur wrapped around it and no bottle. Guess what—the baby used the one with the bottle sometimes and the one with fur at other times. They discovered that the baby needed both!

How amazing! I hate to get sarcastic, but the next time they want to find out something that we already know, maybe they could look at the title of the study and ask themselves whether it has real value.

I often hear about researchers trying to find out why people fall in love. It's okay to ponder the question, but do we need people who are educated and scientifically trained to find out? Do we really want to know? I don't.

Apparently, they wouldn't be embarrassed to tell someone that they were researching falling in love, but they would be ashamed if they said they were investigating an unidentified flying object on a ranch.

NIDS is a standout organization that is brave enough to

look into this. They use objective scientific methodology to prove whatever they encounter—if it's possible.

Colm Kelleher, PhD, is one of the scientists who was there after Tom left the ranch.

NIDS became interested when the story broke, hiring Dr. Kelleher to work at the site that would be set up on the ranch.

The property was bought by Bob Bigelow, a wealthy investor who funded the NIDS operation on the ranch.

By setting up the team to live on site, they hoped to collect evidence that would point in some direction, any direction. The team moved in from 1996–2000. The many bizarre events are recounted in Dr. Kelleher's book *Hunt for the Skinwalker*, co-written with George Knapp.

"Mutes"

One of the first incidences that the team was called to investigate was on the horrific side. Nothing is standardized about cattle mutilation or "mutes."

You couldn't even compare it to a coroner dealing with a shooting victim. With that, you could explain what caused it, when it happened, or at least, make a good guess. Try wrapping logic around this next event.

A defenseless calf splayed out on the ground like trash—its legs pulled off with brutal force and placed on the ground a distance away. Precise slices—removing internal organs and an ear—all done with surgical accuracy, in the span of twenty minutes.

In the late 1970s, cattle mutilations were heavily reported. Due to the inexplicable evidence, speculation was rampant on who or what was involved—and none of it was backed up with evidence.

The team went to perform a necropsy on the most recent

victim—the year-old calf. The carcass was clean—not chewed out, cleaned out. There were no internal organs. The legs were pulled off—torn off with brute force by something and "placed" out of the way at a distance. Another unusual fact was that there was no blood or trail anywhere around the partially snow-covered grounds.

The calf's mother stood back, cautiously keeping her distance after having been a silent witness to the death of her calf.

Tom reported that he had heard nothing of what must have been *extremely* painful. Some people might say, "Well, the blood leaked out of the carcass into the ground."

The team covered that theory, gathering blood from the local "processing plant," in the correct estimated amount. They found a section of ground and poured it around. They left it for the same amount of time, according to Tom, who had agreed to stay on site to help get the team settled.

Even twenty-four hours later, a dark stain could clearly be seen—obvious—from a distance. Whatever did this—and however it happened—the blood had been removed from the scene.

On top of the guided "drone-like" UFO orb and mutilations, the Gormans had many poltergeist-like experiences—doors closing and opening, objects moving to odd locations, etc.

When the Gormans moved in, the first thing they noticed were bolts on the cupboards. The feeling of being watched was a daily stress and the ominous sales contract addendum requested "no digging anywhere on the property" without notifying the former owners.

All these events and many others would never fall under any single explanation that could satisfy the public, the watchful UUFOHs, or a team of scientists.

The Indians had avoided the land for centuries, saying it was cursed. NIDS is gone now. I have no explanation. Maybe cursed is the best we can do. One final note—a photograph taken by Dave Rosenfeld (UUFOH) of the ranch house, at night, with an open shutter, and no flash, came out looking like a firestorm glowing from the house.

A little bit about Skinwalkers—they are, by definition, a witch, Indian, and male. Not many whites had ever been familiar with the term until a few years ago. For a long time, only Indians knew and used it.

Skinwalkers are considered serious business among the Navaho and Ute tribes. They are very evil and the tribes don't like the attention drawn by Hollywood. They have the ability, according to tribal members, to shape-shift and they develop animal characteristics. Often seen around or on a reservation, they have great powers.

A woman in Arizona reported seeing a man-wolf with a shirt and pants keeping pace alongside her truck after trying to rip the door off to get in. She was with her child in the desert. They were both very scared, but managed to get to safety at the next convenience store.

On the Gorman ranch, a beast-like creature—maybe thought to be a Bigfoot—was seen looking in the window of the ranch house. Dr. Kelleher wrote about the ranch in *Hunt for the Skinwalker*. I recommend reading it.

There may be a connection between Bigfoot and Skinwalkers. Many Bigfoot sightings have occurred on reservations, but they've also occurred in many other areas. A nearby canyon—referred to as Dark Canyon—is restricted to whites; even Utes have to receive tribal permission. Petroglyphs in this cursed canyon depict a Skinwalker—among other things we may never discover.

"Canyon of Dreams"

"Canyon of dreams" is the way that Dave Rosenfeld describes the Utah canyon where he has had a lot of UFO sightings. He's taken many great pictures to back it up. Dave is the director of the UUFOHs and his Web site has photos and videos of all kinds that prove he knows what he's doing with a camera.

He doesn't want to give away the location to spoil the chance to get a landmark picture. A photo of a UFO at Wolf Creek was offered to NIDS for analysis. Unfortunately, it came back inconclusive.

Based in Emigration Canyon—because that is where a lot of action of the paranormal kind happens—he drives a monster truck painted with a tiger camouflage pattern and a lift kit for the big rocks.

Magna, 1951

On a clear, warm, summer evening in 1951, all that Audy Harrison wanted to do—like most fourteen-year-olds—was find an ice cream stand. Their neighborhood was at the foothills of the Ochre Mountains at the west side of Salt Lake Valley. It was after eight o'clock and the sun was starting to fade on a clear blue sky—except for one contrail that caught his eye.

It appeared that the lone jet had flames coming out of the tail end. It was definitely red. "Maybe it was the sun reflecting off the exhaust vapor," Audy said. His buddy also couldn't see any wings as it streamed along at airline altitude from east to west. It flew on for a minute. Then, at a sharp degree, it pulled a U-turn and covered the distance it traveled back east in less than a second.

He told me the next day in the schoolroom and a particularly close-minded teacher couldn't resist making a joke out of what the boys had seen. However, they weren't the only ones looking up that night in Magna. A neighbor, Ruth Richards, had seen the same thing and called the newspaper. An article was printed about it.

Utah Crash Site?

Linda Moulton Howe is a writer and investigator with twenty years of experience. Her Web site has a 1953 aerial photo of southern Utah that she says may be the site of a large UFO crash.

The image appears to be a large triangular imprint in a soft sand-gravel mix. She gives no exact location, but since Utah is full of hostile desert, don't expect to find it anytime soon. Her source said that the craft had already been removed from that location by the military.

The UUFOH's website is listed in the back of this book, the photo can be found under "crash sites."

I have no idea whether this is a crash site or not, but if you think Roswell was the only one, think again. Roswell is the most famous crash. There have been less-documented crashes such as Kecksburg, Pennsylvania, in 1965 and Shag Harbor, Nova Scotia, in 1967.

CHAPTER 3
Big Feet

The Northern Utah Encounter

Logan Pond had an eerie feeling. My friend Dave sensed it after I pointed out the lack of tracks around the pond he was about to take a drink out of. In addition, there were no ambient sounds such as birds or trees waving in the wind.

We reached the shepherd's shack after climbing through a valley and some ridges from Brigham City. The pond water was probably safe—it was fed by a natural spring—but something was still strange.

We decided to head back down. We'd hiked there for grouse and, as we stared down a ridge with brush on it, Dave heard some grouse up ahead. I removed the single-barrel shotgun from my pack and assembled it for him. I handed him a couple of shells.

I told him that I'd start down the side of the ridge, but would wait until he was in position. After walking only a short distance, Dave was in a thicket over his head.

He lurched forward to break free and caught his arm on a

branch. He shouted in pain. It was at that point when I heard a sound I'll never forget. It was as though someone had dropped a very large rock into deep water—*bowwwllunk.*

Dave, preoccupied with his stuck arm, apparently hadn't heard it. I looked up and saw "it" running toward Dave's location. Maybe five hundred yards and closing fast, it was large, hairy, and ran like a man.

Yelling loudly for Dave to get out of there, I heard him crash through as fast as he could. The creature kept moving at full speed toward him and I was getting a little scared. Dave could hear it too.

I kept yelling. Dave's thrashing reached a frantic point and his shotgun fired into the air—his only shot.

I looked back uphill for the creature. It had turned around and was heading for the woods. Sweating and shaking, Dave stumbled from the thicket and I eased the shotgun from his hands for safety.

We headed down to the cars together. Dave said that he couldn't even feel the thorns until he got clear and he never got a look at it. I estimated the distance to be five hundred yards or more, but it was closing the distance quickly. From what I saw through the binoculars, it had reddish brown hair and a patch of white on top.

Dave and I didn't really feel like talking about the incident for a couple of weeks.

The preceding was a report of a 1976 encounter that was filed with the Bigfoot Research Organization (BFRO).

The witness was an experienced woodsman and hunter with many years in the woods on his own. The weather had been fair and clear. Nothing had seemed amiss until they reached the old shepherd's cabin.

Sasquatch in Utah

Many Utahns don't realize that there have been as many sightings in our state as in Washington and Oregon—about 160. Many hotspots include Big Cottonwood and Little Cottonwood Canyons, the Logan and Ogden areas, and the high Uintah. There have been a few sightings in Utah's more arid southern regions.

One researcher not only has plaster casts, but also found one that is three-toed! Apparently, Bigfoot is an omnivore, eating rabbits or stolen pigs as well as plants. Don't be put off by this first account. Sasquatch has been seen from as close as eight feet, which is close enough for the startled witnesses.

Boulder Attack

This is another close encounter in the large Cache Valley National Forest. The weather was beautiful as he made his way up the trail. He had been keeping quiet so as not to disturb any wildlife. After crossing the Ogden River and heading east, he started to hear a deep, loud cry up ahead.

After stopping and trying to locate the source and failing, he continued. The sound is described as close to "*huuuurrruuuuu.*"

As the noise repeated louder, he quietly saw where it was coming from. The steep slope in front of him had a patch of thick shrubs and trees in the middle and he suddenly felt that he was being watched.

He decided to make some noise to let the animal know he was there. *Maybe it is a moose,* he thought. That was the only animal that came to mind.

Whatever it was, it knew that he was there watching him—and it wanted him to go. Suddenly, he saw two boulders the size of a basketball rolling down the slope away from the spot where the sounds had come. Nothing inside the brush clump could be seen.

That was all he needed. He quietly turned and headed back down—only feeling relief once he had turned the bend. Whatever this creature was, he really felt it did not want him there.

This man's story had been a secret. He never told his wife of many years, but he finally reported it to the BFRO after more than a decade.

The Patterson Film

Virtually everyone is familiar with the Roger Patterson film made in 1967 of a Bigfoot walking into the woods in Pine Bluff, California.

The area had had prior reports of Sasquatch tracks before Roger Patterson and Bob Gimlin headed out on horseback to search for evidence. They arrived and very shortly afterward, spotted a large biped striding into a stand of tall timber. It was swinging its arms with its steps and looking back at the cameramen.

Some people (who haven't even studied it) think the film is bogus. A British company tried to debunk it in the late 1990s. In a simple side-by-side comparison, the new footage failed miserably—even though the show claimed "victory." Using today's modern effects, they couldn't make a superior film, which would have had much less to work with if the 1967 original were a fake.

No one—*no one*—has produced a costume used in the original footage. No one has come forward as the cameraman or a stuntman wearing the suit.

Every expert who has studied the film has said it's either proof of an undiscovered species or inconclusive.

If you're interested, *Sasquatch: Legend Meets Science*

is a methodical analysis of the Patterson film from an anthropological, aural, and photographic perspective.

The Lagoon Screamer

Ear-piercing, bloodcurdling screams for a week—that's what brought them all outside.

"These screams were louder and higher than a human would scream." The five boys, all from the Centerville and Farmington areas, gathered near Lagoon, Utah's oldest amusement park. It was nighttime in a field near a power plant. The first scream cut the air and the boys ran with flashlights ready to check out the source.

Scared elk bleated as they ran past Lagoon's animal cages. In the clearing, they couldn't see anything, but as they moved back down the trail, they heard another loud scream. They returned to the field and saw a large shape in some trees moving downhill away from them before it disappeared.

On the way back toward Lagoon, they encountered a putrid smell that they hadn't smelled before. The elk and the buffalo now huddled together in a corner.

Then, directly in front of them, the loudest, closest scream filled the air. They couldn't see anything because all of the flashlights were behind the group.

They bolted back to the house. After a month passed, they never heard the screams again.

Why did the screaming last a month and why wasn't it ever heard again? The shape they saw was upright and very tall. This time they claimed to see its eyes—maybe because it was moving away. The foul odor was gone with the screams, but the screams will always be in those boys' memories.

Flaming Gorge National Forest

A brother and sister set up camp at the Flaming Gorge Campground, noticing nothing unusual on their first night. The cows mooing were an annoyance, but they noticed nothing else. The second night was a bit quieter and, by morning, not even the occasional chipmunk was heard. Carl (not his real name) heard two distinct whoops at approximately seven o'clock. His sister was still asleep, but he had heard them. He couldn't relate them to any bird he'd heard before. After listening to audio files on the BFRO Web site of sounds and calls, he thought he heard the same type of "whoop."

The Encounter at LeBaron Reservoir

On a sunny July 4, a couple planned to get away from the main camping area at Fish Lake National Forest in Beaver County. The increasing crowds pushed them farther away.

After camping on a Wednesday and seeing no one for two days, they enjoyed hiking and fishing in a peaceful setting. The morning was pleasant and a perfect sixty-five degrees with a warm breeze. He fished while she relaxed among a few pines that lined the lake.

At about two o'clock, he saw a bear drinking from the water's edge, two hundred yards from his position. He alerted his girlfriend and she reacted with the same level of nervous wonderment. Then it abruptly stood upright and began to walk away from the edge and up the hill.

"Holy sh#t!"

He bolted in shock. His brain ran what he saw through every conceivable North American animal, but none matched the muscular, brown, hairy, upright walking biped that seemed to be weaving to see something ahead of it. It made its way into the woods and disappeared. Their dog had watched the entire event and was silent. He and his frazzled girlfriend hastily grabbed everything and left. They never returned to the area.

They believe that they saw a Bigfoot and their report stated that it was around six or seven feet tall. It didn't see them—or didn't care.

A Cry in East Canyon

A man and his son were on a camping trip in Morgan County near East Canyon Reservoir. The man's mother-in-law lived nearby and said that she always heard loud screams from the rolling hills and surrounding canyons.

Now, out camping with his son, he heard the proof for himself. Through the night, he heard screams lasting fifteen seconds or so.

"I can't imagine a person making such a loud scream," he said.

Many of those screams had low growls in between and even "hoot" sounds were reported that night.

"It can be quite an intimidating sound to hear—especially at night."

They echoed through the canyon, making it hard to gauge the distance. The family had been hearing those sounds for a decade and the father, an experienced hunter, was familiar with common animal sounds.

A Gathering in a Meadow

In a secluded area—roughly seventeen miles north of Ogden and not far from Elizabeth Lake—two couples from Bountiful and Hill Air Force base saw something no one else ever has. I will call them the "Smiths" and the "Moores." Their real names are registered with the BFRO.

The couples were scouting a ridge for future hunting trips. Overlooking a meadow, they saw *three* "creatures" romping in playful antics together.

From an estimated five hundred yards of unobstructed view, four sober, attentive witnesses watched from their hidden spot as two human-like creatures covered with fur walked into the meadow, while a third—probably a hundred yards away—watched or maybe "watched out."

The three creatures never got down on all fours, but ran very fast in large strides across the field.

As usual, they were tall—seven or eight feet was their estimate. Stated plainly, he could've shot one with a high-powered rifle if it was an elk. Their heads were rounded in shape; they had no long snouts as bears do; and their arms and legs were larger than human limbs.

Watching for a while and not really frightened from their relatively safe vantage point, the couples gazed ahead in stunned silence. All three creatures were in plain sight most of the time. Unfortunately, they left their rifles and cameras at home, only packing pistols on this scouting mission. They had no desire to pursue them into darkening woods. Interviewed separately, all the stories were the same. Their families were not told and they didn't talk about it for a while.

After another story was reported from a mother in the Ogden area, they decided they could share their own story.

Startled Scouts

Something about Utah full moons makes them appear larger. A troop of Boy Scouts was out on a merit badge mission under a classic Utah full moon. High in Summit County near Scow Lake, walking along a stream, a couple of boys saw something fifty feet away—it was clearly not human or a monkey—walking along the other side.

The scout assumed that the leader must have seen it, but he was humming a tune and didn't hear it. This creature walked smoothly and fluidly for being seven feet tall. Muscles moved as it went up ahead and made a small "clack" sound crossing the stream, like "stones striking each other." That's when the lead stopped and wondered almost aloud about what was ahead.

They all stopped. It passed very close and it didn't respond to a friendly "hey"—a simple, common greeting among campers and scouts.

Giving another try, they called and waited for a response, but there was no answer. They decided to wait for it to leave. Extremely scared, they waited, collecting odd sticks for weapons in case they were necessary. The creature finally passed around 10:00 o'clock and they cautiously turned and headed back down the trail.

The scout who got a detailed look said that it was "heavy, but not fat, firm, yet stocky," and able to glide along without the effort you might think it would take for a large body over rough terrain. The color of the beast, as best he could make out, was dark brown. The next day they completed what they came up to do. Afterward, they hoped to check for tracks, but rain had washed away any evidence.

The Monster at 12,000 Feet

Many people like to climb Utah's high mountains. The Timpanogos is a 12,000-foot mountain not that far from the famous Sundance resort. Three men had "topped out" and had begun their descent. Still above the tree line and glancing back to see the summit and sunset one last time, they saw a lone dark figure climbing upward at a brisk pace.

They had seen no one on the way down and no one up there. The creature was mostly black or dark brown with no clothing. It was climbing tirelessly through deep snow at a pace that no man could match. It was six to seven feet tall. It would be plain crazy for any man to ascend at the end of the day. The hip-deep snow would have exhausted anyone. The sun would soon snuff out on the horizon and a man would lose his way and begin to freeze to death.

What they saw had no discernable neck and was always moving upright. They know that they saw a Bigfoot creature on the Timpanogos' upper glacier.

South Weber Scare

Ronald Smith arrived home late from the late shift. The moon was full and he thought he'd take a minute to feed the horses. The only thing that he noticed was the sound of something moving around in the shadows of the property. The next day, tracks in the snow indicated a size-fifteen foot. Even stranger was a smaller set of tracks beside the original.

A pair of boys followed the second set of tracks that meandered off toward the barn, fenced off by barbed wire. Hunters that check barbed wire fences at suspected deer crossings often find hair caught on them. Upon closer inspection, the boys found some hair and went to see Sterling Gardner, a judge at the Weber State crime lab.

The 1980 results were "inconclusive," but too much was happening in the small, quiet town of South Weber for anyone to ignore. Why all the activity in such a short span? Who knows?

Myrna Ray burned the stew, but it was no big deal. She put the pan outside on the porch's unofficial "cooling area," only to have it swiped by someone.

Later, the pot was found in the field—licked clean—and large human-like prints were found all over.

Pauline Markham was more than startled to see a large

upright, walking, hair-covered creature swinging its arms as it walked along the canal at 2:30 in the broad daylight.

A sickly stench wafting through town added a potent reminder of the tense mood and jangled nerves already put to the test. Bigfoot researchers arrived from Oregon and Washington, newspaper reporters were asking questions of god-fearing small-town folk, and schoolchildren buzzed with wonder.

Doors got locked and dogs were unnaturally quiet. A lot of people had an eerie feeling that something was in their town and they didn't know why.

Finally, after what seemed like an eternity—but was only about a week—the town was no longer "hot." Things settled back to their normal routine, but no one who went through it ever forgot what they saw, smelled, or sensed.

Monument Valley Sighting

They didn't know what they were looking at, but it wasn't human. It was between seven and nine feet tall, white as snow, and standing among tall rocks. Bob had been leading hikers through southern Utah's gulch area for fifteen years. The area between Utah's southern national parks—Zion, Bryce, Escalante, and Capitol Reef area—was dubbed by *Outside* magazine as the most wild in the contiguous U.S.

Dotted with scrub tree gullies and even cliff dwellings, it is an outdoor enthusiasts' paradise at 5,000 feet.

Looking up as the group hiked along a trail, they all saw it at once. It was a calm afternoon and the blue sky revealed a creature in stark relief. Covered with white hair, it stood among tall boulders that created a fortress effect. It peered impatiently away from the group and reached up often to shade its eyes. The creature didn't see them for fifteen minutes, so they all got good looks. It paced anxiously around inside the stone "turret."

It continually looked away until it turned and spotted them. Then it darted its head and shoulders behind a rock.

The troop of climbers was headed in its direction, but the area where the "albino" monster was happened to be accessible only to skilled climbers.

Not knowing exactly what they were dealing with, Bob decided to change course. Other factors affected this decision—including a lack of water and the time of day—so they turned and headed back toward Deer Creek.

They all sensed that they were being watched as they made their way down, but they all felt a bit relieved.

South Weber, 1980

In northern Utah, Bob Cranston thought the loud crunching sound in the snow behind him in the pasture was a prowler or a high school student. He turned to look and saw someone or something striding toward some clustered trees in his pasture.

It was nighttime and the moonlight shone bright enough for him to see a large person or something possibly in a big parka just make it to the trees.

Suddenly, four loud screams in rapid succession broke the quiet atmosphere. Bob entered his house, hastily I assume, and again heard cougar-like screams. However, these were different and they stopped for a while. Coming back outside later to check on his horse, he found him by the barn, looking calmly toward the trees in the pasture. Cranston asked his wife and neighbors if they had heard anything, but they hadn't.

The next day, looking for tracks in the pasture only produced some shapeless melted prints—*not* made by his horse. He saw indistinguishable one-and-a-half-foot-long tracks that were eight to nine feet apart. Smith decided not to contact the police because of a lack of evidence.

CHAPTER 4
BEYOND HERE BE DRAGONS!

"The Captain and the Devil Fish," maybe that was Captain William Budge's journal entry title that he kept while seeking the beast of Bear Lake.

The captain was a pure Mormon pioneer and had two companions assisting him after they had witnessed a shape rise slowly from the lake. It was shaped almost like a fox on a graceful four or five foot neck.

The eyes were striking and almost set at the same width as a "common cow." It turned—not frantically, but smoothly—at a steady pace out toward deep water. Another odd detail was the coating of murky tan fur on the beast. Its ears were visible even at a distance before its final dive.

William Budge was a well-respected leader of wagon trains and seemed the perfect fit to investigate this unknown creature. With the help of his two witnesses, he made careful journal entries. He also successfully contacted Brigham Young.

In his correspondence, he and Orlando Pratt and Brother Bankhead coined it "The Bear Lake Monster." Latter Day Saint Leaders backed him up enough to finance a hunt for the creature—the same one seen by another man, an apostle in the Mormon Church named George Cannon.

The creature had always been seen by the Indians and was described in simple terms as the "Devil Fish."

It wasn't long after the Budge sighting that Brigham Young, one of the famous cofounders of Salt Lake City, contacted Phineas Cook of Swan Creek to be his "Ahab."

Cook was given a long coil of one-inch rope and solid hooks with orders to catch the beast. Cook got some lamb and made a large bobber float topped with an American flag. The bait was secured to the bobber and the rope to the tree. Now, they waited.

After a while, the bait turned up missing, but Cook had no news for Young. After the end of a diligent, yet uneventful "monster season," Cook sent a message saying he "did not succeed."

The Shoshone

The Native Americans of Utah's five main tribes have a rich history and insight into our past that has not been recorded. They use oral traditions to tell the next generations and they tell the next, and so on.

The Shoshone of Bear Lake have some amazing accounts of a large creature that moves around Bear Lake called the "Devil Fish." It had been known to grab Indian bathers or fishermen from the waters and dive back in. However, the Shoshone say that they haven't seen any sign of the monster since the buffalo left, which was in the 1820s. Did the Shoshone actually see the last of a dying species?

On a warm summer morning in 1871, Milando Pratt and Thomas Rich were hunting on the edge of Bear Lake. However, any ducks that they had hoped to shoot as they walked had flown the coop, traveling with the breeze—or had been scared away by something.

Splashing on the surface got their attention. With guns raised, they watched for a duck or goose, but instead they saw something very long and dark.

Each barrel blasted a 12-gauge round. Both men snapped the single-shot actions and with the smooth precision that comes with much practice, they shouldered and fired again.

The smoke cleared, but whatever it was had slipped into deeper water and disappeared

Loch Ness, 1934

Loch Ness became famous due to the buzz around a photograph that was released showing the profile of a serpentine dinosaur-style head sticking out of the water. The photo was presented to the newspaper by a physician named Kenneth Wilson—and that is the partial reason the claim had so much weight.

Oddly, this photo was proven a fraud by someone who not only believed in the existence of the Loch Monster, but who had a sighting of his own in 1979.

The man researched the photo and talked to a man who knew something unique about this photo. It wasn't just a shot of a silhouette, but it was part of a larger shot including some shoreline of the Loch in the background.

Since it was originally published only once with the background, the later reference shots were all cropped. The only person who would have known there was a background was the man who had taken the photo sixty years earlier (this was 1994).

The researcher suspected this and asked if he had been in on a hoax. Since he was on his deathbed, he said that he and another man had created the creature. They were acquainted with the doctor. Unfortunately, this would get twisted around for the rest of the 1990s as a confession of someone who created the Patterson film—or the Bigfoot film of 1967—but there was no such confession.

The Last Dragon of Stansbury Island

It was an amazing sight to see the dragon flying with the sun glistening off its side and wings as it caught the light.

It was a real—there is no other way to say it—dragon. The creature was so real that salt pellets crumbled and dropped to the ground when it glided overhead.

In 1903, the *Dawson Daily News* reported that Martin Gilbert and John Barry were hunting on the island when they encountered something from another world—a fable creature.

Described as a combination of a "bat, alligator, and fish," it had long jaws and a snout several feet long, his whole body covered in scales that were encrusted with a thick layer of lake salt. They couldn't believe the sight of this creature swirling in slow circles on the clear day.

Its large wings caught the sun and one of the men reflexively tried a shot with his 44-magnum rifle. The shell appeared to hit the target and the creature gave the type of bellow or cry that they'd never heard before—or since.

This flying anomaly landed some miles away and north of their position as they were walking along the west side of the island. They moved quickly to the north to follow.

Large tracks of a five-toed print were not difficult to find. It almost resembled a "hand nearly four feet across the palm."

The trail led to an ominous cave on the north side. Caution and fear guided their next move—to not enter its lair—and build a blind to hide in and observe.

Using several large flat stones, they constructed a narrow and somewhat camouflaged hiding spot. They climbed in and waited. As the sun finally began to set, the creature could be heard shuffling toward the entrance from less than twenty feet away. They saw that it had a head ten feet in length, a body around sixty-five feet in length, and a very thick crust of salt on its scaly hide.

Its front legs were smaller than its back legs and its wings flexed. After a short sprint, its hundred-foot wingspan caught the air and it glided off, flapping higher and higher. The young moon was a wavering dot rising on the lake's surface as they waited fearfully for the return of the creature. Torn between wanting to leave and needing to stay, their decision was made for them as the creature returned. In its mouth was a large horse. It had been swooped upon, they imagined, and crushed in the dragon's powerful jaws.

The dragon carried the horse into the cave and settled down to a meal. The men heard a loud crunching of bones coming from inside the dark inner cave. Gilbert and Barry slipped away to their camp on the eastern shore for the rest of the night.

The next day seemed calm enough. As they were about to launch their boat, they saw the dragon thrashing and diving in the water. Thinking quickly, they eased the boat upside down on the shore and crawled underneath it. From fifty yards away, they watched the dragon feeding or chasing something in the water (possibly brine shrimp).They noticed that its eyes seemed unaffected by the salt concentration—they were possibly protected by a clear lid.

This went on for about half an hour. The dragon dove briskly and eventually ended up around the distant point to the north.

The men were relieved when they emerged from their hiding spot and returned to Salt Lake City. They told their tale—with even more details than presented here—to the *Dawson Daily News*.

This, of course, reads like a fairy tale, but the original

account in the paper had even more detail than was necessary. The men didn't seem to make any fortune from their story.

What if they saw the last beast of which fables were born? The first accounts of ostriches and Komodo dragons were probably met with skepticism early on. Where did it go? Remember that it did have wings. A short time later, trappers followed a large something through an area of the very wild Yukon.

CHAPTER 5
CRYPTIDS

Their truck bounced along a northwestern road in Utah's Mahogany area. Joe Martin and his son were watching for deer.

Joe spotted a large black figure sitting on the rocks about a hundred yards away. He was on the verge of pointing out a black bear to his son—even though there are not supposed to be that many black bears in the western desert areas.

It was not moving at all and was about four to five feet tall. Suddenly it spread its large wings and leaped upward. It climbed into the air quickly with a strong wing thrust. Mr. Martin estimated the wingspan around fourteen feet.

The experienced hunter thought that it must be some kind of anomaly Golden Eagle, but realistically, even that would be a stretch. The Golden Eagle stands at forty inches with a wingspan of only seventy-eight inches.

What he may have seen was what Indians have referred to as "Chenemeke,"or "Hahness", but the white man used the term "Thunderbird."

They got this name from the legends of large birds moving on the winds carrying a thunderstorm. It goes without saying that they can shoot lightning out of their eyes and thunder out of other places.

Not only Native Americans, but in modern times, there have been many sightings by people in several states, but mainly in the eastern half of the country.

There have been sightings from Pennsylvania to Illinois and as far away as Alaska. They are bigger in description than even the largest known bird, the Wandering Albatross, which has a wingspan of twelve feet. However, the Wandering Albatross lives in an ocean environment.

The Thunderbird (some estimates describe a twenty-five-foot wingspan) is either very rare, very shy, or both; it may be on the brink of extinction. When you venture out, I recommend bringing a camera, not a cell phone with a built-in camera.

The Utah Kangaroo

Ray Ault may have taken some ribbing over his story, but he is sticking to it.

On a clear, dry day on his Cedar Fort ranch in 1981, he was out checking the fences and sheep. The rancher turned from a fence and saw something that should not have been there. A kangaroo was staring at him. It quickly leaped six feet into the air and trotted off toward the hills. Ray had seen photos and TV shows and knew this was a real kangaroo. He recognized the yellow and brown coat—an excellent color for camouflage in Utah or Australia. The climates aren't that different, so it follows that a kangaroo may survive a while, but how did it get here?

CHAPTER 6
Crop Circles

Crop circles are all over the place—England, Japan, China, India, and of course, Utah. They can be complex and amazingly beautiful. The majority of them, however, are phony. Andrew Collins, a British researcher, estimates that 80 percent are manmade, but the other 20 percent remain unexplained.

I have a few ideas about what might cause the unexplained ones, but none of them are solid. The Beehive State has had six in the last decade. There are ways to investigate and authenticate them. Investigators take photos, seed samples, stalk samples, and earth samples for evidence, just as at a crime scene. They even record sound and video in case there's something that may help explain what they were dealing with.

As if crop circles weren't mysterious enough, add in the balls of light (B.O.L.) that have been seen and recorded on video—in England mainly. They may somehow be connected to these events, along with the strange sounds and atmospheric pressure changes that are felt as soon as one walks into a circle. Colors are often altered and a small number of people even feel nauseous in a freshly discovered crop circle. The effects are greatly reduced when they return at a later date.

Colin Andrews also caught the British military helicopters (sometimes referred to as "Black" helicopters) and B.O.L.'s in the area of a crop circle reacting to each other. Why does the military care if people are visiting crop circles? Does it have something to do with the validity of a formation?

A Circle in Ice

To add another curve to the already twisted path in these investigations is a very unusual ice circle formation found in February on a ranch in northeastern Utah. The sheriff, a retired NIDS investigator, was on the scene in forty-five minutes to view the ice circle.

A simple and virtually perfect circle was carved or sliced into the ice. No footprints were found in the mud, save for cow prints. Who—or whatever—carved the circle did so on a thin sheet of ice during the night.

Investigators estimated that the ice was three-quarters of an inch thick and could possibly support fifteen to twenty pounds. The diameter measurement was five feet nine and the depth was one-quarter of an inch deep. Upon noticing shavings along the ring, that evidence removed speculation of heat being used. Shavings of ice were collected and analyzed, but no abnormalities were found. This tiny unnoticed occurrence is even more unexplainable than other circles.

CHAPTER 7
CHEMTRAILS IN OUR SKY

Have you ever looked up on a clear blue day and seen trails of white smoke crisscrossing and slowly evaporating?

Where are all those planes going? It seems that on many days—over every major city in America—more than just airline traffic is marking the sky.

These are often referred to as contrails—streaks of condensed water vapor that trail planes at high altitude.

"Chemtrails" are different. They are chemicals sprayed by planes of all types at any altitude. They are different in what they contain and how long they linger. This category includes crop dusters, mosquito spraying, and planes dumping extra fuel before landing.

A chemtrail-observing community believes that it could be a large-scale government operation of unknown motive.

Now, before you start thinking I'm paranoid, read on.

When I interviewed Audy Harrison about a UFO he had seen, he told me about another event that happened during World War II. His outfit was told (not asked) to get in line for a shot. He did what he was told, just as the others did. During the next week, they were all sick. The following week, they were told to go get another shot.

When it was his turn, Audy said to the doctor, "You gave us something. What was it?"

"Don't worry about it. You don't need to know," said the doctor.

Audy replied, "You can't do that to us."

"We can do anything we want. We're the government."

That is one example of the military-industrial complex that President Eisenhower feared and spoke of. A government that had to become powerful enough to defeat Germany and Japan may have become too powerful and unaccountable to anyone.

Sometimes citizens report strange smells and minor illnesses during these lingering web works of smoke.

I don't suggest that anyone should panic, but noticing chemtrail activity on a casual basis might be a start. If you notice high activity, you could always find out who is up there. You could use a Web site that has an Internet-based flight-tracking tool called "Flight Explorer." It shows same-day flight activity—although it will not identify military flights for security reasons. This site is listed at the back of this book.

Since there are unidentifiable military planes crisscrossing the sky creating a substance film that lingers for twenty to sixty minutes over a population, you've got the right to wonder about it.

CHAPTER 8
Deep Underground

Many supposed conspiracy theorists focus on the underground tunnels and bases in Utah and much of the information is available through the Freedom of Information Act (FOIA).

Were you aware that Utah contains 67.9 percent of the known underground bases acreage—and they are federally owned?

In Utah, there is a mountain storage facility for Latter Day Saints' records in Little Cottonwood Canyon—it is safe from earthquakes and fire.

I would doubt that such an elaborate and "serious" level of protection goes in a hundred feet and stops. This must be a massive project with several levels—and it even has a tunnel that leads all the way to Salt Lake City.

Other reports and legends exist about a massive grid of tunnels under the city; some people claim there are thirty miles of tunnels. A former security guard and his friend discovered a tunnel in the lower level of the late-great Crossroads Mall, located downtown. They actually went through three "small rooms" down to lower levels that he wasn't supposed to enter. They finally stopped at a horizontal tunnel entrance that was over two hundred feet long; it was strung with lights and had two men in suits packing Uzis. They decided not to go in, backed out, and went down to two more block rooms and found a manhole cover with "HZ" on it and a tunnel big enough for a semi.

The technology to build a tunnel large enough to drive a truck through is fairly easily done—and has been for a while. You may have heard of the Yucca Mountain underground storage for nuclear waste in Nevada and the Cheyenne Mountain Base in Colorado, a military base for thirty years that is strong enough to take a nuclear blast.

Proof of an underground base in Utah may be thin, but there are plenty of tunnels, dams, and reservoirs.

Whether Dugway Military Proving Grounds have deep underground sections is highly probable. If I ran a military base, I would definitely take advantage of tunnel technology and build down. If there are underground tunnels, could bases be far behind? On the other hand, what about a top-secret baseball diamond? Before I go crazy on the possibilities, it would be very practical to store facilities of military needs such as weapons, R&D projects, and laboratories.

The technology has been around for decades, and you'd be surprised how much can be done. Boston's Big Dig is an example of simply bad engineering.

What about tunneling under the ocean floor? Could it be possible someday? If you go to Japan, you can ride a train in a tunnel between Honshu and Hokkaido. It is thirty-three miles long with fourteen miles that slope down beneath the ocean floor—over 700 feet beneath the ocean floor! It's the deepest railway tunnel in the world. According to the experts, digging tunnels is "child's play."

Several companies manufacture tunnel bore machines (TBMs) in Japan, U.S., Russia, and England. We have government agencies that have programs for this work, such as the Department of Energy, the Navy, and the Army Corps of Engineers.

It stands to reason that if a lot of information about tunnels is available through the Freedom of Information Act, then we know they are a reality. What's to stop an agency from making secret underground bases?

You might ask how a tunnel operation could be carried out without suspicion. Tunnel operations can be camouflaged to look like traditional mine sites. Dirt from the sites could be stored in buildings and even distributed in groundwater and spring run-off through tunnels. "Road construction" nearby could even distribute the extra material. Ventilation could be created by having a shack on the surface—not a shack, but actually a ventilation port.

Anyone with enough money can buy his or her own TBM—the TBM exchange international will sell you one— you just need $700,000 to $2,000,000 and you'd have to be able to afford the shipping cost for a 186-ton vehicle. You could then carve your own mountain retreat/storage unit/ secret hideout.

Does anyone think Area 51 is a group of hangars? Obviously, the government doesn't pour billions into just that. It's safe to assume that it goes underground five to ten floors— and maybe more. It makes sense. If you've got the budget and can't build out, you build down.

CHAPTER 9
Ancient Lands and Modern Man

Most paleoanthropologists can compile a timeline with great confidence. It goes from the start of early life in the Cambrian age—long before mammals—to primates, Neanderthal to Cro-Magnons, and modern humans, etc. evolution runs through its core—except, of course, the missing link. But why is that evidence still missing?

Earth, 300 million years ago, teemed with prehistoric life known as trilobites (marine arthropods). They were common crab-like creatures that were found everywhere—especially in the yet-to-be-named Antelope Springs, Utah. Today, these fossils sell in gift stores in Moab, Park City, and all over the state.

A fossil is similar to an imprint in concrete—except concrete sets, or becomes solid, much faster. The thing that makes the Antelope Springs fossil interesting is the human shoeprint that has been apparently fossilized *with* the trilobite. If that is the case, it proves man has been on earth much earlier than estimated.

The trilobites date back 500 to 600 million years. Was man walking around in Cambrian shale?

William Meister first discovered it in 1968. He was an amateur collector and trained draftsman who discovered the fossils when he broke open a block of shale.

This fossil flies in the face of the accepted timeframe of life on earth. Therefore, it's often dismissed out of hand by scientists who haven't even examined it—even though the footprint is alone and not in a sequence. It never deviates from the shape and pressure of a manmade shoe.

Gadianton's Dimensional Curtain

In the 1870s, a canyon not too far from the Utah-Nevada border was feared due to a terrorist brotherhood called "Gadianton," which according to the book of Mormon, sprang from the Nephites and Lamanites a century before Christ. The freighters who ventured the slick rock canyon with supplies bound for Pioche, Nevada, told stories of the cult of assassins that lurked there—and even canyon walls literally "closing around them." Over time, stories faded around campfires in Utah's Iron County—until the spring of 1972 when four coeds from Southern Utah University were returning from a rodeo in Pioche.

It was around ten o'clock and the girls wanted to make it back to Cedar City and their dorm room in time for their curfew.

They had crossed the border into Utah about nine miles west of Modena. They drove steadily along Highway 56—a desolate stretch of highway that cuts through sagebrush and cactus with a line of sandstone cliffs to the north.

Janna North was trying to be careful with her dad's year-old Chevy Nova. The engine hummed along while the girls chatted. They steadily watched the Modena landscape and the railroad tracks that crossed through the small town. Just beyond the tracks, Janna noticed something odd. Instead of the one road, two now branched off. One veered north into the desert and the other led to the southeast.

"Which one do we take?" asked Carol.

"Left," Janna said.

She probably figured that it was a shortcut through the canyon and would save them time getting back home. Only a few minutes later, the Chevy cruised into a canyon unlike any other.

After driving only a short time, they noticed that the highway changed from dark pavement with a centerline to light-colored concrete.

Suddenly Carol shouted, "Janna, up ahead!"

Carol braced as Janna hit the brakes and skidded to a stop. The concrete they were on went directly into a sheer face of red rock cliff. Janna complained about the lack of warning signs as she backed the car up and steered onto the road.

"Can we even make our curfew now?" asked Lisa.

Tension began to set in with each passenger. They became quiet and focused as they tried to piece things together. They should have been out of the canyon by then.

Internal sighs of relief must have welled as the canyon walls broke and the scenery changed in the moonlight. A new source of unease made an appearance—wavy fields of grain and a lake were to the left, along with tall stands of Ponderosa pine.

"This sure ain't Modena," said awestruck Carol.

"We must've gotten turned around back there," offered Janna cautiously. "Where the hell are we?"

They approached what looked to be a roadhouse—complete with the standard neon sign—but it was only a series of squiggles. There was a driveway next to it and Janna decided to turn around in it. As she slowed to pull onto the dirt driveway, they saw a group of agitated men leaving the building.

"There are some guys," Carol said.

Bethany giggled and asked, "Are they cute?"

"Let's find out," Lisa said, cranking down the passenger window.

"Lisa, we don't have time for this," Janna warned.

Lisa quickly touched up her lipstick in the mirror and said, "Relax. I'm only going to ask how to get to the highway."

There seemed to be great agitation among the men as they approached the car—as though they were startled by some strange animal.

Lisa stuck her head out the window and hollered, "Hi, we're—"

At that fleeting moment, Lisa screamed in terror.

Janna lurched in her seat and yelled, "Lisa, what?"

"Get out of here!" Lisa yelled as she desperately cranked up the window. "Punch it, Janna!"

"Step on it!" cried Bethany.

Tires blasted sand as the Chevy lunged onto the road and spun away from the building. Looking back in the mirror, a bizarre scene confronted Janna.

"Oh, my God, they're coming after us!"

Stepping down hard on the gas pedal, the lake flew by on their left.

Behind them, four vehicles were closing in fast—the likes of which they'd never seen and would never forget. Four egg-shaped vehicles buzzed along on three wheels and single glaring orb headlights.

"Janna, faster! They're getting closer!"

The road led back to the canyon and they were again surrounded by red rock flashing by at eighty miles per hour.

Janna kept her eyes on the road and tried not to look back. She was sweating as the cliffs seemed to crowd the blacktop. Their pursuers had broken away from view and they soon shot out into familiar desert. Without warning, the road disappeared and their headlights shined only on sagebrush and desert hills.

They were bumped and tossed hard as Janna tried to brake, but the car slid sideways down an embankment and ground to a dust-enshrouded halt. Trembling with adrenaline, each girl slowly emerged from the battered Nova, surprisingly unharmed. The car had taken the worst of the injuries—three flat tires, many dents, scratches, and a missing hubcap.

Janna looked over the once-proud muscle car and said, "My dad's gonna kill me!"

Lisa, however, was more affected by having seen their pursuers than the others.

She sat, holding her knees and crying, "They weren't human!"

Not daring to leave the car, they waited until the sun rose above the cliffs and walked south until they came to the highway. They were lucky to wave down a Utah Highway Patrol officer after only a short time.

The ensuing investigation by Trooper Vic Lundquist and a few volunteers who scoured the area resulted in some puzzling questions. Tire tracks from the Chevy could only be followed back two hundred yards. There were no tire tracks showing where they had left Highway 56 in Modena. Despite a thorough search, the right hubcap was never found.

Is there a thin area in dimensions where people and things can temporarily pass through? Is the canyon a warp entranceway? Maybe the four "beings" who chased the girls are pondering the only proof of their story—a very strange object, the missing hubcap.

There are other examples of "timeline anomalies" that scientists have yet to explain, such as the metallic vase blasted out of a construction site rock. The bell-shaped metal contained some silver and had been broken in half by the blasting. Marks on the side skillfully inlaid with silver depicted a flower and bouquet.

This was no hoax. It was imbedded in solid pudding stone and is dated around 600 million years old. That puts fine metalworkers in North America when life was supposedly just forming.

Belgium has stone tools carved by the earliest modern hunters between 25 and 38 million years ago, according to the Oligocene period sediment they were found in.

In South Africa, metallic spheres have been found by the hundreds in a mine. Each one of the orbs was made of a hard metal that is difficult to scratch—even with steel. The equator is circled by three equally spaced parallel grooves that help date these orbs to 2.8 billion years ago.

Texas has the Taylor Trail. A drought revealed a riverbed and the fossils in it—dinosaur tracks moving in a straight line and human footprints going in the same direction mixed with them. Stan Taylor found it in 1967, eventually uncovering fourteen sequential human prints and 134 dinosaur tracks from tons of limestone.

Pole Shifts

Pole shifts in the past have been thought to be only magnetic, where the earth's magnetic poles actually change their position, true north flips to the South Pole and all south magnetic readings are in the north. Geologists using a radiosotopic method to measure magnetic properties in ancient rock can calculate when the magnetic field changed. A shift hasn't happened in thousands of years.

The other theory is the earths crust actually moved on the surface like a high speed continental drift, with land masses causing violent change for life here.

It would explain other anomalies such as mammoths being found flash frozen with flowers in their stomachs. Mammoths were not creatures of the arctic climate anyway and having flowers from a temperate zone has always been hard to explain away. However, the arctic has a huge stockpile of mammoth tusks that pose the question.

A map residing in the Library of Congress shows the coast of Antarctica in detail; the map was made four hundred years ago.

An ancient text tells an old Indian story of a "Mahabharata" war with a huge fireball and a mushroom-shaped cloud. Elephant's miles away were knocked off their feet and the sand in the area melted, turning to green glass.

Jenny Randles coined a term in *Timestorms*, noting several incidents of people "jumping" great distances or maybe through time.

In most of her books' cases, there is a cloudy apparition in the atmosphere and the smell of electrical burning. Then, people end up either down the street in a neighbor's garden—bewildered and walking unsteadily home—or on another continent completely without explanation.

What if a civilization was ground under and we started again, several times? So-called "men of science" who push aside—and even hide—facts that don't fit are not scientists. Their job is to study evidence and record it accurately—not to force and toss pieces of history to make the puzzle fit.

CHAPTER 10

Dark Highways

All highways are given a number designation. These numbers carry a lot of beliefs and controversy surrounds them.

The 666 is a number like any other, designated for a stretch of highway that happens to be normal road—or one that runs through the devil's own backyard.

Imagine driving through a dark southeastern Utah landscape and seeing what looks to be a fire moving on the road toward you from the distance. It gets brighter as it gets closer and you pull off the road to be safe, moving quite far over on the pull-off. Then a semi-truck engulfed in flames surges past like a freight train and continues down the road.

From a little girl's ghost who walks the side of the road to the "devil dogs" seen running in packs along the roadside, what happens on the road stays on the road.

The Highway 666 runs from western Colorado into Utah and runs south, southeast, and down toward the Four Corners area.

A few years ago, the Utah Department of Transportation changed the number designation to Highway 191. If you change the name of a cursed highway, would it be as dark?

CHAPTER 11
Adventures with the U.U.F.O.H.'S

Alien Dave e-mailed me about the Dugway Skywatch and I immediately wanted to go. Knowing that we were going out to rugged desert about an hour west of the city, I decided to rent a car instead of using my own.

I finished drinking my coffee while I waited on a quiet road a few miles from Antelope Springs for the caravan to meet up. Three cars turned and I saw the infamous "Dave Mobile." It was a tiger-striped Jimmy with an open top and a lift kit, along with a row of spotlights lining the top of the windshield.

We got out, greeted each other, and met the German film crew that came along. They were filming a story on our group for their television show back home called "Inside USA." After talking a while and deciding what they wanted for shots, they set up. Matt, a U.U.F.O.H., rode with me.

Matt is a good guy. We talked on the way to Dugway's eastern side along Antelope Springs parking area for ATVs and whatnot. The parking lot actually bustled with activity that day.

The view of Dugway is good. It's surrounded by a large

area with some half-exposed debris in the sand. We climbed up to a rock outcropping about three hundred feet up, so we had a good perch to film from and discuss the area.

We went back to the parking lot for the other half of our trip, circling around to the Northern side of Dugway, known as the knolls.

The road runs north to south along the fence on Dugway property, which explains how they will "use lethal force" if they need to (they seriously will). The Germans got some shots of the fence signs. No one came out to harass us, so we decided to continue, but we had to wait for a half minute for a herd of antelope to cross the road.

We briefly got to I-80 and drove west for a little while before cutting another left south onto the knolls road. This is where I regret not renting an SUV. Dave was the only one of us really prepared for this kind of road.

The Germans occasionally hung out of their minivan to get some "in caravan" shots and did some running to get a distant passing shot.

The sun was sinking low and we followed close. We reached the plateau after avoiding numerous large stones and potholes and then made the final do-or-die climb up over the ledge.

The view looking mainly east presents more fence and more signs, which we posed next to with the grinning Germans. We waited and watched. It got dark and cold—really cold. Dave fired up the stove and we gathered round for a tailgate party.

Off to the north, a continuous pearl strand of car lights told me that Wendover—a split-in-half border town for Nevada and Utah that is jam-packed with casinos—will never go out of business.

Crowded around the fire, the Germans asked the last of their questions, shot their film, said goodbye, and headed out. The early hour and nasty wind chill urged us to call it a night at three o'clock. I followed the other cars closely because one wrong turn in that scrub and you could end up in a "bad place." I made my way to the nearest McDonald's for a cup of coffee.

On a later Dugway Skywatch that I didn't make it to, Dave got photographs of a "beam" that shot straight up into the night sky. Several team members experienced minor side effects such as nausea and headaches. His photo and story made the local nightly news.

CHAPTER 12
STUFF YOU CAN DO

You can usually find out about the paranormal areas where you live through the newspaper. On the Web, you can search for sites, but www.aliendave.com is great for local strange happenings in Utah. For more general and precise topics, you can try one of the many sites being added to the Internet every day.

You can ask anyone you know—or even a librarian.

Ghost tours are given every Halloween in Salt Lake City and Ogden.

UFO information can be found anywhere on the web. It's the second-most-searched subject next to sex.

Hit a Convention

You can feel more involved and supported—or simply have fun at conventions. One of the best known is the "UFO Congress" held for the past fifteen years in the Aquarius Hotel in Laughlin, Nevada. You can keep up on a number of interesting issues during the weeklong marathon of speakers and films. You can browse the exhibit floor and buy a couple of hard-to-find books .

The speakers' presentations are very professional and the banquets before the dinner are elegant. It is very well organized and features well-known speakers (in UFO-ology) every year.

On the night of the banquet, I happened to be fortunate to have the keynote speaker, Richard Dolan, at our table. He wrote the comprehensive book, *UFOs and the Security State.* Although he is serious about his subject of study, he's also very funny.

In addition, there was Rob Simone, an L.A. radio personality, author, and busy speaker. Between Richard and Rob, our table was the most fun—especially if you were tired of hearing about Republicans and Democrats.

I have no affiliation with the Aquarius Hotel. It's a pretty nice place and there are many activities that you can occupy spare time with if you don't like gambling—jet skiing, boating, fishing, or walking through ghost towns.

Following Bigfoot

On the Web, you can find out about Bigfoot conferences by going to these websites.
Texas Bigfoot Research Conservancy, http://texasbigfoot.org/
The Bigfoot Conference, Salt Fork State Park and Wildlife Area, Ohio. http://www.angelfire.com/oh/ohiobigfoot/abchtml

Equipment You Should Get

Buy a camera—a good digital camera is the way to start. It's one of the few things you can buy that is going up in quality and down in price.

A digital tape recorder is handy in case you are listening to a strange whoop or scream in the dark woods or out in the middle of nowhere.

The G.I.S. has a great Web site. They are a local group of ghost hunters and their Web site has information on equipment that is more specialized to their field. There are also digital recorders, infrared cameras, temperature scanners, and such.

Ghost Investigation Society, http://www.ghostpic.com/index-6.htm

Join a local group of Bigfoot researchers if that is your focus or start a group of your own.

In other words, groups can be a great way to get involved. MUFON—the Mutual UFO Network—has *free* meetings every month. Find them and get their meeting info on the Web.

If you live in Utah, become a member of the Utah UFO Hunters. You can then go on one of the many "skywatches" (going out usually at night to observe any unusual activity). They plan the trips or you can plan one for the group yourself.

On a hike, bring binoculars, a camera, and a buddy. Four eyes are better than two.

Look up at the night sky as people have done for millions of years and watch and wonder. If you don't see anything but stars and the occasional satellite, at least your blood pressure will go down, and you'll get a sense of the vastness of the universe.

Bibliography

Chorvinsky, Mark. *True Reports of the Strange and Unknown.* Lakeville: Fate Magazine, November 2002.

Coleman, Loren. *Mysterious America.* Winchester: Faber & Faber, Inc., 1983.

Cremo, Michael A., and Richard Thompson. *The Hidden History of the Human Race.* Los Angeles: Bhaktivedanta Book Publishing Inc., 1996.

Good, Timothy. *Above Top Secret: The Worldwide UFO Cover-up.* New York City: William Morrow and Company, Inc., 1988.

Hauck, Dennis William. *Haunted Places, Ghostly Abodes, Sacred Sites, UFO Landings, and Other Supernatural Locations.* New York City: Penguin Group, 1994.

Jones, Marie D. *PSIence: How New Discoveries in Quantum Physics and New Science May Explain the Existence of the Paranormal Phenomena.* Franklin Lakes: The Career Press, Inc., 2007.

Kelleher, Colm A. PhD., and George Knapp. *Hunt for the Skinwalker: Science Confronts the Unexplained at a Remote Utah Ranch in Utah.* New York City: Pocket Books, 2005.

Kermeen, Frances. *Ghostly Encounters: True Stories of America's Haunted Inns and Hotels.* New York City: Warner Books, 2002.

Randles, Jenny. *Time Storms: Amazing Evidence for Time Warps, Space Rifts, and Time Travel.* New York City: Berkley Books, 2001.

Salisbury, Frank. *The Utah UFO Display.* Old Greenwich: Devin-Adair Co., 1974.

Sauder, Richard, PhD. *Underwater and Underground Bases.* Kempton: Adventures Unlimited Press, 2001.

White, John. *Pole Shift.* Virginia Beach: A.R.E. Press, 1980.

The Utah U.F.O. Hunters, http://www.aliendave.com/

The Bigfoot Field Researchers Organization, http://www.bfro.net/

The Ghost Investigators Society, http://www.ghostpix.com/index-6htm

Coast to Coast am, home of paranormal radio, http://www.coasttocoastam.com/

Cryptomundo, Bigfoot and unknown creature website, http://www.cryptomundo.com/

Gadianton Canyon Time/warp, article by Branton, http://www.rense.com/general/utah.htm

Breinigsville, PA USA
02 March 2011
256739BV00001B/68/P